Practical Pet Care

HAMSTERS

Printed and Bound in China

06 07 08 09 10   1 3 5 7 9 8 6 4 2

Library of Congress Cataloging-in-Publication Data
Hamsters / TFH experts.
p. cm.
Includes bibliographical references and index.
ISBN 978-07938-1009-3 (alk. paper)
1. Hamsters as pets. I. T.F.H. Publications, Inc.
SF459.H3H54 2006
636.935'6--dc22
2006026353

This book has been published with the intent to provide accurate and authoritative information in regard to the subject matter within. While every precaution has been taken in preparation of this book, the author and publisher expressly disclaim responsibility for any errors, omissions, or adverse effects arising from the use or application of the information contained herein. The

Hamsters enjoy manufactured treats such as this nut roll, but small quantities of fresh fruit, such as apple, or vegetables are better for them.

techniques and suggestions are used at the reader's discretion and are not to be considered a substitute for veterinary care. If you suspect a medical problem, consult your veterinarian.

The Leader In Responsible Animal Care For Over 50 Years!™
www.tfh.com

CONTENTS

Introducing Hamsters

Understanding where hamsters come from and how they live

There are 27 species and subspecies of hamster found in different countries and habitats – as well as many color, pattern, and coat varieties – but only five of these are regularly kept as pets. By far the most common is the Syrian hamster, also known as the Golden hamster (Mesocricetus auratus). At 6–8 in (15–20 cm), the Syrian hamster is also the largest of the pet species. The other four species – Russian Dwarf Campbell, Russian Dwarf Winter White, Roborovski, and Chinese – are also featured in this book (see pages 20–25). All make ideal pets, though the smaller varieties are best kept by adults or older children.

WHY KEEP HAMSTERS?

Hamsters are among the most popular small pets in the world– and not without good reason. They are:

- **entertaining** – their inquisitive and playful nature means that they are great fun to watch and play with.
- **friendly** – if acquired at a young age, a hamster is easy to tame.
- **clean** – hamsters don't smell, provided you clean their cages and replace their bedding regularly.
- **small** – they don't take up much room, which means that they're suitable pets even where space is very limited.
- **inexpensive** – after the initial cost of providing suitable accommodation for them, hamsters are relatively cheap to maintain.

The first pet hamsters

The Golden Syrian is still the most commonly available pet hamster.

The Syrian hamster was the first hamster species to be kept as a pet. It was first discovered in 1839. But Syrian hamsters were believed to be extinct in the wild until a female and her young were captured at Aleppo, Syria, in 1930. They were taken to the Hebrew University in Jerusalem, where some were bred and their descendants were later imported into the US and UK. They were originally used in laboratories, but were introduced to the pet market in 1945. Hamsters have since become one of the most popular pets throughout the world.

Understanding Your Hamster – how he lives

Gaining an insight into how hamsters live in the wild will help you to understand and care for your pet better. A new hamster that nips you, for example, is probably not being aggressive. Until he learns to recognize your smell, he probably thinks your fingers are for eating!

Wash your hands!
Because hamsters rely on their sense of smell rather than sight close up, it is important to wash any potentially alarming smells from your hands before you feed or handle your hamster.

Hamsters in the wild

Wild hamsters are found in Eastern Europe, the Middle East, and Asia. In the wild, they often live in deserts where they make their homes in burrows consisting of tunnels and chambers. Although they are not strictly subterranean – they forage above ground for food – they spend most of the daylight hours underground to avoid predators and the fierce daytime heat and extreme cold of winter that are typical of the desert climate.

Food is hard to come by, and hamsters must search for seeds, nuts, and plants to eat. Hoarding is a characteristic of all hamsters (the word "hamster" comes from the German word *hamstern*, which means to hoard). Most species have cheek pouches in which they transport the "hoard" back home. Hamsters have adapted to need very little water and can survive on the small droplets of dew that form at the entrance of their burrows in the early morning.

The Syrian hamster can carry up to half his body weight in food in his cheek pouches.

The hamster's senses

Of all his senses, the hamster relies primarily on his sense of smell, using his nose to "see" his environment, other hamsters, and people.

Like most small mammals, hamsters are far-sighted, which enables them to spot predators at a distance in the wild. Their

Hamsters have very acute hearing, which means that their ears will be sensitive to loud noises. Make sure that you keep your pet's cage in a quiet room.

close-up vision, on the other hand, is very poor, which means that your hamster may not be able to distinguish your fingers from titbits, which may lead to a few nips until he learns to recognize your smell.

Another essential tool for small prey animals is an acute sense of hearing, and your hamster will soon learn to recognize your voice and to distinguish it from that of strangers. Once he learns to associate hearing your voice with receiving food, your hamster may come out of his nest when you call.

Hamsters are far-sighted, so your hamster will be able to smell but not see you at close quarters.

Hamsters rely primarily on smell to provide them with information about their environment.

The hamster's body clock

Hamsters are generally described as nocturnal, but in fact they are crepuscular – they come out in the evening and early morning. This makes them ideal pets because they sleep most of the day and wake up around the time when the human family comes home. It is important to respect their sleeping hours, and a new hamster, in particular, should be allowed to choose when he wakes up.

Hamsters may react to cold conditions by falling into a deep, coma-like sleep – a form of short-term hibernation. The body temperature drops, the heartbeat slows down, and breathing is imperceptible. Exposed to warmer temperatures, a hibernating hamster will gradually surface.

tip

Don't rush to bury a "dead" hamster

If you find your hamster cold and stiff in the middle of winter, place the cage in a warmer room in case he is not dead but sleeping.

Hamster language

Most of the time, hamsters don't make any noises audible to human ears. Take note of any vocal language, as it probably means that your hamster is upset. Your hamster will communicate

Although hamsters sleep for much of the day, they usually wake up in the mornings and evenings.

WHAT IS YOUR HAMSTER SAYING?

You hear...	Your hamster is...
a series of squeaks	expressing irritation
squeaks interspersed with soft grunts	angry
teeth-chattering	issuing a warning
piercing shrieks	terrified

tip

Give your hamster space
If your hamster makes noises, he is probably frightened and should be left alone. Be particularly sensitive to a new hamster and give him time to settle down.

Hamsters are fast runners and love exploring. They are also great escape artists, so make sure you close the cage door properly!

much more to you in his body language, and you will soon be able to tell when he is feeling relaxed, curious, friendly, defensive, or tense.

Exploring and climbing

All hamsters, particularly the dwarf species, can be very active once awake and particularly enjoy tunneling and climbing – though they are better at climbing up than down! You will need to provide suitable play equipment for your hamster, learn how to handle him properly and catch him if he escapes, and provide a safe environment for him if you allow him out of the cage. (For more information, see pages 44–51.)

The hamster's paws are extremely dexterous and versatile. He uses his feet not only for climbing but also for holding his food and to groom himself.

Hamster Species and Varieties

Choosing which species and reviewing the colors

Although the most commonly kept hamster, the Syrian, is still often called the Golden hamster, breeders have now developed numerous other color varieties, as well as many other patterns and coat types. Four other species of hamster – all dwarf species – are available as pets, but they have different care requirements from their Syrian relatives. Dwarf species are sociable and can be kept in pairs or colonies; they can be less friendly, harder to handle, and are much faster moving than the Syrian.

Syrian, or Golden, hamster

Check housing needs

Remember that Syrian hamsters must be kept on their own, whereas all the dwarf species can be kept in a pair or group, though only with others of the same species.

CHOOSING A HAMSTER

Hamster species	Characteristics/availability	Care requirements/potential problems
Syrian (or Golden)	Readily available in numerous different color varieties, patterns, and coat types. The largest species of pet hamster.	The most suitable for young children. Must be kept as individual specimens only: if you want to keep more than one, you will need more than one cage.
Russian Dwarf Campbell	Most commonly available dwarf species (often listed simply as "Russian" in pet shops). Many colors and two pattern types are now available.	Can be kept as a pair or in a group. Can be nippy. Commonly suffer from diabetes. Occasionally afflicted with glaucoma.
Russian Dwarf Winter White (or Siberian)	Currently the hardest species to obtain in pet shops. Three colors are available.	Can be kept as a pair or in a group, though squabbling between individuals can occur. More tolerant to being handled than Campbells, but still not an ideal choice for children.
Roborovski	Unequaled in entertainment value, and they spend more daylight hours awake than other species. Only the normal color is currently available.	Will be happy kept as an individual, but can also be housed in pairs or groups. Less likely to bite than other dwarf species, but they are very fast movers and therefore unsuitable for children.
Chinese	Often very shy, but love tunneling and climbing and are therefore entertaining to watch. Slightly harder to obtain than some other dwarf species. Limited choice of colors.	Can be kept as a pair or in a group, though squabbles can occur between mature adults.

Syrian Hamsters – color varieties

The Syrian hamster was originally known as, and is still often called, the "Golden hamster." Golden is the original wild coloration, but breeders have developed many other color varieties, as well as patterns and coat types (see pages 16–19) since the first hamsters were kept as pets.

Hamster colors fall into two categories, selfs and agoutis. A self-colored hamster will have the same coloration throughout and no markings. (Some self-colored hamsters may have a small white line under the chin, a small spot of white on the belly, and an area of white just above each foot. These "socks" are more prominent on darker self-colored animals.) Self colors include cream, white, ivory, black, sable, mink, chocolate, and dove.

An agouti hamster will have a multi-colored coat with markings. Agoutis have two stripes of color on the sides of their face and head. These stripes are called cheek flashes and crescents. The hairs on an agouti will often be two-toned in appearance, with more than one color on each strand. For example, the cinnamon-colored hamster has an orange top coat, but the roots of the hairs are grey. Agouti colors include golden, cinnamon, dark grey, silver grey, yellow, and honey.

Both self- and agouti-colored hamsters are available in patterned forms (see pages 16–17).

1

2

3

1: yellow. 2: red-eyed cream. 3: melanistic yellow (yellow black). 4: golden (daughter), golden satin (mother). 5: chocolate. 6: chocolate (sable). 7: long-haired golden. 8: blond banded.

TOP 10 COLOR VARIETIES

Some of the colors shown on the following pages are difficult to obtain, but the following popular colors are generally available from pet shops:
- *golden*
- *white*
- *black-eyed cream*
- *red-eyed cream*
- *cinnamon*
- *sable*
- *honey*
- *yellow*
- *black*
- *mink*

4

6

5

7

8

1

2

3

4

5

6

7

1: black-eyed cream. 2: dove dominant
spot. 3: golden 4: black.
5: mink. 6: long-haired flesh-eared
white female (left) and male (right).
7: silver grey. 8: cinnamon.
9: smoke pearl. 10: cream (juvenile –
color will darken with age).

8

9

10

LONG-NAMED HAMSTERS

All the hamster colors can be mixed with
different patterns and coat types –
sometimes with more than one of each.
A hamster variety name will be formed
of the color, the pattern, and the coat
type. The animal shown here may look like
a tailless white mouse, but she's actually
a dark-eyed ivory dominant-spot long-
haired satin female Syrian hamster!

Syrian Hamsters – patterns

As well as the many colored hamster varieties, there are also several common types of pattern that occur in hamsters. As with coat types (see pages 18–19), a hamster may show more than one of these patterns, and all may occur on self- or agouti-colored hamsters (see page 12). Indeed, a hamster may exhibit both a pattern and a coat texture; for example, you could have a satin dominant-spotted hamster.

Banded

The ideal banded hamster will have a white belly and a complete white band encircling the middle third of his back. In many banded hamsters, however, the white band is incomplete, failing to meet in the middle of the back, or it may be a thin ring or take up most of the body. As with other patterns, this can be combined with any color.

Black Banded

Cinnamon Dominant Spot

Dominant Spot

Hamsters with this pattern are mainly white with spots of another color. Although the ideal dominant spot is one that is evenly spotted all over the back, some dominant spot hamsters may have large patches of color rather than spots and some may not look spotted at all. All have a white belly and white blaze on the face.

Black Tortoiseshell

Tortoiseshell

This bi-colored hamster is produced using the sex-linked yellow, so that a golden tortoiseshell is golden with varying amounts of yellow patches in his coat. The tortoiseshell and white hamster is similar, but with an added white color and can be produced with many of the colors, the most striking of which is undoubtedly the black tortoiseshell and white. All tortoiseshell hamsters are female.

Umbrous

The gene that causes the umbrous pattern mutation is often called the "sooty gene" because it makes an otherwise standard-colored animal look as though he has been rolled in soot. For example, the umbrous golden is a dark golden with grey crescents and belly, almost as if the Golden hamster has had a grey wash placed over his normal color.

Roan

The coat of a roan hamster is white with coloured hairs ticked through. These coloured hairs are often concentrated around the head and the amount of colouring on the body can vary from one hamster to another.

Silver Roan

Don't mate roan to roan

Never mate two Roans together as they will produce white hamsters with very small eyes or even with no eyes at all. (See Breeding Hamsters, page 63).

Syrian Hamsters – coat types

Syrian hamsters are available in two coat lengths, short haired and long haired, and also two types of coat textures, rex, and satin. It is possible to have more than one variety of coat on the same hamster; for example, you could have a long-haired satin hamster or a short-haired satin rex.

Short-haired hamsters

Short hair is the original wild coat type. Short-haired hamsters should have a short, dense coat where the fur lies flat to the body. It is possible to have both rex and satin coat textures in short-haired hamsters. The short-haired coat will appear the same on a both sexes.

Long-haired hamsters

The long-haired hamster originated in America, where it was called the Angora. In the US, these hamsters are often also known as Teddy hamsters because of their cuddly, fluffy appearance.

The coat on a long-haired male and female will appear different: only males have the very long tresses. Female long-haired hamsters have a coat that is only slightly longer and fluffier than that of the short-haired variety.

*Long-haired
Golden female*

Groom long-haired hamsters

Hamsters with very long hair are not equipped to groom so much fur themselves and need brushing regularly to prevent their their coats from becoming a tangled, matted mess.

Long-haired males can have very long coats that will require regular grooming.

Satin-coated hamsters

The coat of these hamsters has a highly shiny appearance. Like rexes (see below), satin-coated hamsters can produce stock with coat problems: satins mated to other satins will produce offspring with very thin fur.

Yellow Satin

Rex-coated hamsters

On rex hamsters, the hairs are lifted and slightly curled. This gives the coat a soft plush appearance in short-haired hamsters and a wavy coat in the long-haired ones. Long-haired male rexes can look a little scruffy. The whiskers of a rex are also curled. Early rexes were plagued with a poor coat, and this problem sometimes recurs. The rex first appeared in 1970.

Long-haired Sable Rex

PASTEL OR BRILLIANT?

Colors can vary depending on the type of coat. Both long-haired and rex coats will make the color of a hamster paler than in the normal, short-coated version. These dilute colors appear soft and are often very attractive. In contrast, the satin coat tends to increase the depth of coloring.

Dwarf Hamsters

In recent years, several dwarf species of hamster have become available to pet owners. As we've seen, these smaller hamsters are less suitable as pets for young children than the Syrian hamster because they are much faster moving and harder to handle. Also, as they generally prefer to live in pairs or colonies, any mistake you make in sexing your hamsters (see page 35) can leave you overrun with babies. They can also be quite quarrelsome. However, they are delightful to watch and so can make entertaining pets for older children and adults.

Russian Dwarf Campbell

This is the most commonly available dwarf species and will often be seen for sale simply as "Russian" in pet shops. Like other dwarf species, it can be kept singly, in a pair, or as a colony of single-sex or

The Russian Dwarf Campbell is the most commonly available dwarf hamster species.

Platinum Russian Dwarf Campbell

mixed-sex individuals, although owners should be aware that squabbles can occur.

The normal color of the Russian Dwarf Campbell has a brownish-grey topcoat with a dark grey undercolor, a dark, brown-grey dorsal stripe, and an ivory belly. There should be three arches on the side separating the top color and belly color, and these arches have a rich creamy tint. The eyes are black, and the ears dark grey. Argente and albino Campbells are quite commonly available, and other colors have also been developed, for example dove, black, and black-eyed white.

The are also two main patterns: mottled hamsters are patched with white, while platinums have white hairs intermingled with their colored hairs, which gives a silvering appearance to their color.

Albino Russian Dwarf Campbell

Mottled Russian Dwarf Campbell

Normal Russian Dwarf Campbell

MALE OR FEMALE?

There may be no real difference in temperament between the sexes of Russian Dwarf Campbells, but many experienced owners consider males to be easier to keep together than females. Females in a group will often try to establish themselves as the matriarch of the colony, and this can lead to squabbling.

tip *Buy Campbells with care*
Your Campbell should be bought from a reputable source as diabetes is quite common in this species.

Russian Dwarf Winter White

Also known as the Siberian, this relative of the Russian Dwarf Campbell is much less commonly available. Despite its name, the normal color of winter white is actually dark grey with an almost black undercolor, a black dorsal stripe, and an ivory belly. The species derives its name from the fact that in the wild, although it is dark in the summer, it has the ability to molt to a winter white coat that camouflages it in the snow.

Sapphire Russian Dwarf Winter White

The Winter White shares many characteristics, as well as common ancestry, with the Campbell. Both are fond of exercising (particularly on wheels) and prone to squabble with other hamsters, but the Winter White is more tolerant of being handled.

In addition to the normal color there is a sapphire form, which has a smoky blue-grey coat with grey dorsal stripe, black eyes, and grey ears.

Both normal and sapphire colors are available as pearls. Pearls are white animals ticked through with colored hairs, particularly along the back. The normal pearl has black ticking and the sapphire has purple-grey ticking.

tip

Don't confuse the two Russians

Although the Russian Dwarf Campbell and the Russian Dwarf Winter White have a common ancestor, they are separate species, and it is inadvisable to crossbreed them. Hamsters labeled "Russian" in pet shops are likely to be Campbells.

Normal (left) and Normal Pearl (right) Russian Dwarf Winter Whites

Roborovski hamsters

These entertaining little hamsters are the smallest species kept as pets. Robos, as they are commonly known, are becoming more readily available, although there are currently no color varieties. The normal coloring is grey, but turns sandy golden with maturity, with white belly and eyebrows, black eyes, and flesh-colored ears edged with grey.

Roborovski hamsters have lots of energy and tend to spend more daylight time awake than all the other species, much of it playing on their wheel and exploring their cage. Although they are unlikely to bite, and children will enjoy watching their antics, they are not suitable for those who want a cuddly hamster to tame as they move very fast and are easily dropped.

With an average length of 1½–2 in (4–5 cm), these smallest of all pet hamsters are only about a quarter of the size of Syrians.

Like other dwarf hamsters, Robos prefer to be kept in pairs, but they will also live happily on their own.

Chinese hamsters

Chinese hamsters have a mouse-like appearance, with a more prominent tail than other varieties. Indeed, although they are generally referred to as dwarf hamsters, they are officially classed in the group known as rat-like hamsters. Like the other smaller species, they can be kept singly, in pairs, or in groups. They can be quarrelsome though, so you may need to split pairs into separate cages.

The normal form is a brown-grey color with a black stripe down the back and lighter fur on the belly. The only mutation is the dominant spot, which is white with patches of color. The coloring is usually slightly greyer than on the normal.

Chinese hamsters tend to be very shy and will often burrow into their bedding to hide away. As well as being good at tunneling, they are expert climbers, which makes them very entertaining to watch.

The normal coloration of the Chinese hamster is brown-grey. He has lighter fur on his belly and a black stripe along his back.

This dominant spot Chinese hamster is the only other color variety of Chinese hamster. Amounts of white in the coat of this variety can vary.

tip

Don't use a standard wire cage

Chinese hamsters can easily wriggle through the gaps in wire cages made for Syrians. Keep them in an enclosure with glass or plastic sides.

Provide climbing apparatus

tip

Chinese hamsters love to climb, so make sure you equip their cage with a selection of small branches and ropes for them to play with.

Chinese hamsters enjoy tunneling as well as climbing, so provide suitable apparatus for them.

Chinese hamsters can be kept singly, in pairs (either single sex or mixed), or in colonies. However, squabbles can occur, particularly between females, and you may need to separate hamsters if fighting escalates.

Housing Your Hamster

Choosing, furnishing, and locating your hamster's cage

You will need to have a suitable cage and all essential furnishings in place before you bring your new pet home. Your hamster will spend most of his time in his cage, so it is important that you choose the largest one you can afford and have room for. It should be of a sturdy design suitable for the species you want to keep. You will also need to consider where to locate it.

Locating the cage

Remember that hamsters don't sleep at the same time as humans! You will need to choose a peaceful place for the cage and one where your pet's daytime sleep won't be disturbed and where he won't keep you awake at night.

The cage should be placed on a sturdy stand, shelf, or table and not directly on the floor (where it would be within reach of other pets).

The cage should be kept away from direct sun, heaters, and draughts. A comfortable living room temperature suits hamsters well. Never keep hamsters in an unheated room or shed – they may hibernate in cold weather.

EQUIPMENT CHECKLIST

Make sure that you have thought about, chosen, and budgeted for the following:

**Water bottle
(see pages 33 and 40)**

One that attaches to the bars of the cage will provide your hamster with fresh clean water.

**Cage
(see pages 28–31)**

Make sure it is large enough, and remember that some wire ones are unsuitable for smaller species.

**Exercise wheel
(see pages 48–49)**

Some cages come equipped with one, but it may be too small for a Syrian hamster. Solid wheels are better than wire ones, which may hurt or trap a hamster's feet.

**Wood shavings
(see page 32)**

You will need to buy plenty, particularly if the cage has a deep base.

**Food bowl and food
(see pages 33 and 40–43)**

Choose a sturdy bowl so that it can't be easily tipped over and don't forget to buy some hamster food!

Nest box (see page 32)

A variety of types is available: this natural fiber one is warm and cosy.

**Bedding material
(see pages 32–33)**

Your hamster will want soft bedding to line its nest. Buy proprietary nesting material.

**Play apparatus
(see pages 48–49)**

Hamsters love tunneling and climbing so provide suitable playthings.

Hamster Cages – choosing which type

There are many types of hamster cage available. Which you choose will depend on the species you want to keep, whether the cage needs to house one hamster, a pair, or a group, and how much space you have available. The most expensive or prettiest may not necessarily be the best or the most practical. Try to look at the cage from your hamster's point of view and consider his needs.

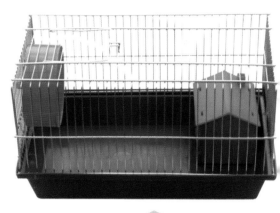

Traditional wire cages

A basic hamster cage will consist of a plastic base and a rigid wire top. Wire cages come in various

A basic hamster cage like this may come complete with a nest box and wheel.

CHOOSING A HAMSTER HOME

Type	Advantages	Disadvantages
Single- or multi-story wire cage	Relatively inexpensive and often comes equipped with wheels, ladders, etc. Easy to keep clean, and hamsters enjoy climbing on the bars.	Spillage of wood shavings, etc. can be a problem, particularly if the base isn't high enough. A cat may be able to reach in. Also, dwarf species may be able to escape through the bars.
Stacking or linking tube system	Can be added to at any time and provides lots of opportunities for the hamster to explore and access different rooms.	Interlinking tubes may be too narrow for large or pregnant Syrian hamsters, and young or nervous ones may hide in the tubes and be difficult to retrieve. Can be hard to clean, and ventilation may also be a problem.
Aquarium-style tank	Safe and relatively easy to clean. Solid sides means there is no spillage of wood shavings, etc. Good visibility.	Ventilation can be a problem (make sure it has a well-ventilated and secure lid). Needs regular cleaning, and it may be heavy to move. Hamsters will need to be provided with climbing apparatus.

sizes, shapes, and colors, and are relatively inexpensive, easy to keep clean, and long lasting. This type of cage is unsuitable if you have a cat, however, as cats can easily hook their claws through the wire.

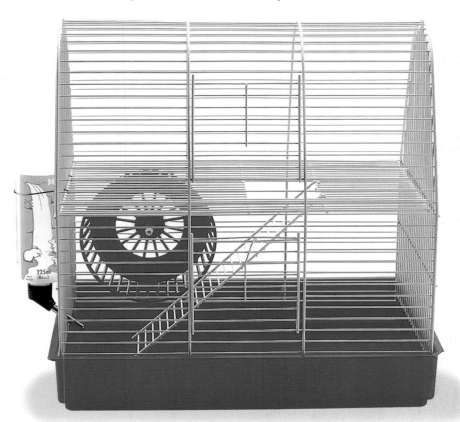

tip

Keep a wire cage away from curtains

Your hamster won't be able to resist adding pieces of your curtains and soft furnishings to his bedding if he can reach them through the bars of his cage!

It is worth picking a two-story cage to provide your hamster with more living space.

Because of the small size of basic models, wire cages are unsuitable for dwarf species, which are very active. In addition, the gaps between the wire bars of a standard hamster cage will be too wide for smaller species, which will easily be able to squeeze through them. Dwarf hamsters may be kept in a cage designed for mice in which the bars are closer together.

Some wire cages have more than one level, with features such as metal or plastic ladders and bridges built into them. Whether you choose a basic or a multi-story model, make sure it has a high base to contain wood shavings for your hamster to burrow into.

Aquarium-style tanks

A glass or plastic aquarium-style tank can make a good home for a hamster. The solid sides contain wood shavings; also, hamsters can't get out and a cat's paws can't reach in. The tank must have a secure, well-ventilated lid and should not be too deep or it will become too hot and stuffy. As ventilation will be more limited, tanks need to be cleaned regularly to prevent them smelling of urine. Make sure that you provide something for your hamster to climb on to make up for the absence of cage bars.

A simple tank-style hamster home like this must include a well-ventilated lid and exercise facilities.

Linking tube systems

Some cage designs incorporate a system of linking or stacking tubes that extend the basic cage and are designed to mimic the wild hamster's burrow. These cages are

A cage formed from units linked with tubes lets a hamster explore and access different "rooms".

CHECKLIST: CHOOSING A CAGE

- Is it big enough? A cage supplied as part of a small starter kit may not be large enough to house an adult Syrian hamster.
- Is it gnaw-proof? Check for vulnerable spots in cage joints and lids or your hamster may be able to chew his way out!
- If you have chosen a wire cage, is the plastic base high enough? If not, wood shavings and food may be kicked out of the cage by the hamster.
- Are the catches attaching a wire cage to its base secure?
- Will you be able to retrieve your hamster from it? Not all multi-story cages have access to all levels, and it can also be difficult to retrieve a nervous hamster from a plastic module cage.
- Is it escape proof? If you want a wire cage and plan to keep dwarf hamsters, check that the gap between the wires is no more than $1/3$ in (8 mm).

more expensive, but you could start with a basic design and add extra compartments as your hamster gets older. They are unsuitable for pregnant or very large Syrian hamsters as they may have difficulty moving through the interconnecting tubes, while dwarf hamsters may encounter problems climbing the vertical tubes in units designed for Syrians.

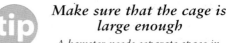

tip

Make sure that the cage is large enough

A hamster needs separate space in his cage for eating, sleeping, playing, and toilet purposes, so the cage should ideally be no smaller than 30 x 12 x 12 in (75 x 30 x 30 cm).

Some interlinking hamster homes are made from plastic rather than wire. Both types can be added to at any time.

Furnishings – getting the cage ready

Hamsters like to have separate areas in their homes for playing, eating, sleeping, and toilet purposes. They are also active and inquisitive and love to have areas to explore. (For more on play and exercise, see pages 48–49.) Before you bring your new hamster home, you will need to make sure the cage contains a sleeping area, plenty of wood shavings, bedding materials, and, of course, food and clean water.

materials, including shredded paper and soft fluffy bedding, from a pet store. Don't be tempted to make your own from cotton wool, tissues, or synthetic fibers, which can be fatal if eaten or if the hamster gets caught up in the material.

Wood shavings

The cage will need to be lined with plenty of wood shavings to give your hamster something in which to burrow and to soak up any wet patches.

Buy these from a pet store: those from other sources may have been treated with chemicals that will be harmful to your hamster. Avoid fine sawdust, which can cause irritation to a hamster's eyes, nose, and lungs.

Nest boxes

Although your hamster may prefer to create his own sleeping area, most appreciate a nest box in which to sleep. Nestboxes for hamsters are available in various designs, materials, and sizes, including two-story ones.

You will also need to provide your hamster with some soft bedding to line his nest. You can buy suitable nesting

Most hamsters appreciate a nest box, which will function as a bedroom and, sometimes, a food larder.

Make a hamster potty
Lay a clean jam jar on its side in your hamster's cage and place a little soiled litter inside to encourage your hamster to use it.

Some hamsters will use wood shavings to line their nest, but most prefer something softer.

Food and water containers

Providing your hamster with a food bowl will help you to keep the cage clean and to ensure that your hamster is not overfed. Sturdy earthenware bowls are best as they are not easily tipped over— buy two, one for dry food and one for fresh.

Supply water to your hamster via a drinking bottle that clips to the outside of the cage bars or attaches to the inside of a plastic or glass tank with suction pads. Those with a ball-bearing in the drinking tube are less inclined to leak, but in any case, avoid suspending the water bottle over the food bowl or your hamster's bed.

Hamster potties

Hamsters are very clean animals and will adopt a separate area of their cage as a toilet. You can make the task of cleaning the cage even simpler by providing a "hamster potty" for your pet. Buy one from your pet store or make one yourself.

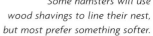

Make sure that the drinking bottle is well within your hamster's reach.

Buying Your Hamster

When and where to buy your hamster and which to choose

Assuming that you have already decided what species to buy and whether you want one, a pair, or a group (see chapter 2), you will still need to consider where to buy your new pet and make sure that you select a healthy hamster – not just a cute one. If you are buying more than one, you will also need to make sure that the hamsters have been sexed or you will soon be overrun with babies!

BEFORE YOU BUY

You will need to consider the following before you buy your new pet:
- If you want more than one hamster and don't want lots of babies, you'll need to make sure that they are of the same sex.
- The average life span of a hamster is only about two years, and this may pose an emotional problem for small children.
- Although children love hamsters, those younger than about eight years old may not be able to handle them with sufficient care.
- Hamsters are easy to maintain, but children will need some supervision in caring for their pet.
- If you or anyone in your family suffers from asthma, borrow a friend's hamster for a few days to make sure you are not allergic to him. Make sure that you choose a short-haired variety.

Male Russian Dwarf Campbell

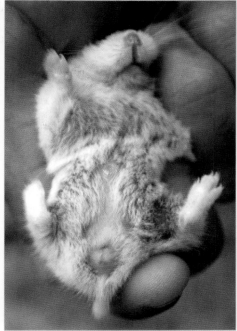

Female Russian Dwarf Campbell

Male or female?

Knowing whether you're buying a male or a female hamster may not be too important if you're only going to buy one as either sex will make a good pet. (Some owners have found male Syrians to be more placid than females, so a male may be a better choice for a first-time petkeeper.)

However, if you want to buy a pair or group of dwarf hamsters – and you are not planning to breed them – you will need to make sure that they are of the same sex or you could soon find yourself overrun with babies!

Males of most hamster species are generally thought to be easier to keep in a single-sex group than females, which have a stronger tendency to fight with each other.

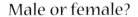

To determine sex, check the distance between anus and genital opening, which is wider in males. Adult males also have a more pointed bottom.

Baby or adult?

Baby hamsters are weaned at three or four weeks and will be ready to go to a new home by the time they are about six weeks old. Young hamsters are harder to sex than adults, but they are easier to tame. You will need more patience if you choose an adult.

tip

Remember that Syrians are solitary

Most small animals will be lonely living on their own, but not the Syrian hamster. If you want two, you will have to keep them in separate cages.

The Right Pet – choosing him and taking him home

It is important that you choose your hamster carefully, and finding a suitable retailer is your first step. Once you've decided where to buy, you'll want to select the right hamster for you and make sure you've picked a healthy one. You will need to have a suitable box or cage in which to transport him home and to have prepared his new home before you buy him so that you can settle him in quickly.

Where to buy your hamster

Most pet shops will have a selection of different hamster varieties for sale. Spend some time observing the animals. They should be kept in clean cages – dirty,

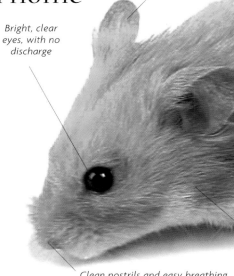

Clean ears

Bright, clear eyes, with no discharge

Clean nostrils and easy breathing

tip

Check his diet
Ask the vendor about the food that your new hamster has been eating and take some home with you.

crowded cages mean potentially sick hamsters – and males and females should be housed separately. (Hamsters breed from a very young age, and you don't want to discover that you've inadvertently bought a pregnant female.)

Staff should be able to answer questions about the hamsters and their care. Do bear in mind that they may have less time to answer questions on busy weekends, though.

Selecting an individual

Although you may have personal preferences as to color and pattern, or may just see an individual that appeals to you, the most important thing to consider is that your new

Children will enjoy helping to choose a new family pet, but make sure that you select a healthy hamster, not just the cutest one!

Shiny fur

Clean tail region

Scent gland may be visible on hip (normal)

Normal cheek pouch

CHOOSING A HEALTHY HAMSTER

pet is healthy. A hamster may be asleep when you come to look at him, but when gently awakened, he should be curious and come out of his nest. If he remains sluggish, he may be ill. Ask the vendor to get him out of his cage so that you can examine him more closely. Check for clear, easy breathing, shiny fur, a clean bottom, and bright, clear eyes.

Taking your new pet home

Most pet shops will supply you with a cardboard box in which to take your new hamster home, or you can bring your own — a large plastic ice cream container with air holes punched in the lid will be ideal. However, it's a good idea to invest in a small carrying case for your pet, which you can also use if you need to take him to the veterinarian and when you are cleaning out his cage.

A plastic carrying case filled with some bedding material or wood shavings is ideal for transporting a new pet home.

Caring for Your Hamster

Enjoying your hamster and keeping him healthy

tip

Don't intrude!
If your new hamster retreats to his nestbox, don't try to retrieve him and respect his privacy. A frightened hamster will probably bite.

Now that you have introduced your hamster to his new home, you will need to spend some time each day providing him with food and water and cleaning his cage. Hamsters are relatively low-maintenance pets, but to enjoy your hamster you will need to learn how to handle him correctly. It takes patience to tame a new hamster enough for him to trust you, but the benefits will be worth the effort and, provided you take suitable precautions, you will eventually be able to allow him out of the cage (see pages 50–51).

The first few days

When you first bring your new hamster home, he will be nervous and will probably go into hiding. Leave him alone, simply providing him with food and water and, after a while, he will come out to explore and have something to eat and drink. Clean the cage when necessary, but move slowly and don't try to pick up the hamster. Speak to him softly so that he becomes accustomed to your voice.

At this early stage, feed only the hamster mix that your pet was used to before you bought him. In particular, avoid feeding fresh foods as very young, newly purchased hamsters can sometimes develop stress-related diarrhea.

A new hamster will be nervous at first; leave him to settle in and he will soon emerge from hiding.

ROUTINE CARE

It is a good idea to establish regular routines for caring for your hamster right from the start: they will help your new pet to settle into his new home and ensure that you don't overlook aspects of his care.

Daily
- Feed your hamster and provide clean water (see pages 40–43). (Check the water bottle for any leaks or blockages.)
- Remove any uneaten perishable food.
- Stroke your hamster or take him out of the cage to encourage him to become tame.
- Remove and replace any soiled bedding and clean out the hamster's "potty" or toilet area (see pages 32–33 and 53).
- Groom a long-haired hamster to prevent his coat from becoming matted (see pages 54–55).

Weekly
- Clean the cage, discarding and replacing wood shavings, soiled bedding, and hoarded food. Wash and disinfect the cage base using a pet-safe disinfectant. (See pages 52–53.)
- Check for any damage to the cage or furnishings.
- Check your hamster for any signs of ill-health (see page 56–59).

Monthly
- Check the hamster's teeth (see page 56).

Feeding – providing a balanced diet

Your hamster will benefit from a varied, nutritionally balanced diet. However, you should start a new hamster on the same mix as he was receiving when you bought him, and change his diet only gradually. Hamsters are hoarders and in order to satisfy your hamster's hoarding instincts, it is important that you feed more food than he needs to eat in one go. Much of this food will be carried off and stored.

The hamster's staple diet

The basis of the hamster's diet should be a mix of grains, seeds, and nuts. Although you can mix your own, it is easier to use a commercial hamster food mix, and doing so will ensure that your pet receives the correct balance of nutrients. (Too many sunflower seeds or peanuts in the mix are fattening.) As an alternative to the traditional seed mixture, you can buy pelleted food or food blocks. About two teaspoons of dried food twice a day should be sufficient.

WATER SUPPLIES

Hamsters that eat more fresh food will obtain most of their liquid intake from their diet. Nevertheless, it is important that they have access to fresh water at all times, so replenish the water bottle daily, even if your hamster doesn't appear to be drinking.

A commercial hamster mix may contain crushed and clipped oats, flaked maize, sunflower seeds, peanuts, dried peas, grass pellets, and dried biscuit.

Keep food dry
Store your hamster's food in a sealed container in hygienic conditions. Avoid food that looks old or dirty.

Offer your hamster no more than one small slice of apple or the equivalent daily.

Pear

Broccoli

Fruit and vegetables

Hamsters enjoy some fresh food, but this is not a daily necessity and should be offered sparingly — diarrhea can result from too much fruit and vegetables in the hamster's diet. One broccoli floret or a slice of apple or carrot is sufficient. Individual hamsters will have their own likes and dislikes, but you could also try feeding the following: sweetcorn, cucumber, broccoli, grapes, bean sprouts, tomato, melon, swede, and cooked potato. Wild foods such as dandelions can be fed in small quantities too.

Make sure that fresh food is of good quality and that you have thoroughly washed it and shaken it dry.

Cabbage

Carrot

Apple

Parsley

Nuts form part of a standard hamster food mix, but also make good treat foods in moderation.

DANGEROUS FOODS

Some fruits and vegetables are bad for hamsters — and some may even prove fatal. Avoid the following:

- leek
- chives
- onion
- garlic
- raw potato
- aubergine

- orange
- lemon
- lime
- grapefruit
- avocado

Protein foods

Contrary to popular belief, hamsters are not vegetarians but omnivores, and they benefit from having some additional protein in their diet. Twice a week, try offering your hamster a slice of hard-boiled egg, a teaspoonful of cottage cheese, scrambled egg or plain yogurt, or a sliver of cooked chicken.

Live foods such as mealworms, crickets, or grasshoppers are also acceptable, two or three at a time. Buy these from a pet shop, and never feed insects from your garden as they may be contaminated with insecticides.

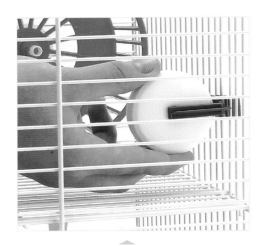

A mineral block will help keep your hamster's teeth healthy. You can buy one from your pet shop that clips to the sides of the cage.

Something to gnaw

Hamsters need to have something to gnaw on to keep their teeth healthy. Wooden

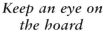

chews are available commercially, but you could also feed your hamster pieces of hard, dry toast or a small dog biscuit once a week, or provide a cuttlefish bone, as sold for budgerigars.

You could also furnish the cage with some small branches. Never use branches that may have been exposed to pesticides, and make sure that there is no mildew or fungus on them. Wood from fruit trees such as apple, pear, plum, hawthorn, and blackthorn is best.

Roughage and supplements

Hamsters need some roughage in their diet, and you can provide this with a handful of oat or timothy hay. Although your hamster may decide to use it for bedding, he will probably still nibble enough to do him good.

If you are feeding a hamster a balanced diet, he shouldn't really need supplements. However, a mineral block will keep teeth healthy as well as providing trace elements.

Keep an eye on the hoard

When you clean the cage, check to see whether your hamster's food store has increased. If it has, reduce the amount you are feeding.

Treats and titbits

Children will enjoy feeding treats to their pet hamsters, but should be discouraged from feeding the types of unhealthy treats that are meant for humans. Treats such as chocolate, fudge, and toffee will not only lead to obesity, but will also clog the hamster's cheek pouches.

Special treats designed for hamsters are available from your pet shop, but remember that these should be fed only as an occasional extra. Healthy treats such as a raisin or a peanut will be enjoyed just as much as manufactured, sweetened titbits.

This special hamster treat provides a tasty snack and welcome exercise for the hamster's teeth.

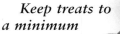

Keep treats to a minimum

Like humans, hamsters suffer from obesity if they eat too many treats, particularly if they are sweetened.

Feeding the occasional treat, such as a peanut, by hand will help your hamster to associate you with pleasurable experiences.

Taming – getting to know each other

Once your hamster has had a few days to settle in and has become accustomed to your voice, you can begin to try to stroke your new pet with one finger. (Avoid stroking his head though, as this seems to make most hamsters nervous.) Don't be alarmed if your hamster tries to nip you – he has to become used to your smell and may just think your finger is food!

Once your hamster seems less nervous, try stroking him gently through the bars of his cage. Move slowly and mind your fingers!

If he appears to be frightened, leave him alone. Let your hamster learn to trust you before you try picking him up, and make all movements slow and gentle to avoid frightening him.

Later you can try putting a treat in your hand and stretching your hand into his cage, but never try to stroke your hamster while he is in his nest box.

How to pick up your hamster

The first time you try to pick up your hamster, approach the cage and talk to him quietly. If he is asleep, tap the cage gently and he should wake up. Always wait until he is out of his nest and facing you before you attempt to pick him up. Hamsters rely a great deal on their sense of smell, so always wash food residues off your hands before handling your pet. You should also always wash your hands afterwards.

As you will need to use both hands to start with, you might find it easiest to remove the top of the cage. Place the whole cage inside a cardboard box first, then remove the top. Cup both hands gently underneath the hamster's body and use a scooping action to lift him up. Don't try to restrain him at this stage, but allow him to run over your hands within the box.

When you lift your hamster out of the box, it is important that you hold him gently but firmly. Hamsters are small, fragile animals, but they can move fast and can wriggle out of a loose grip with ease. Avoid lifting the hamster too high, and keep your hands close to your body.

tip

Sit down while holding your hamster

In order to prevent falls and injuries, sit down while holding your pet and make sure he is facing you.

To start with, use both hands to
pick up your hamster, cupping them
gently underneath his body.

By placing one hand in front of the
other, you can encourage your hamster
to walk across them.

Once tame, your hamster will enjoy sitting in your hands. Facing a new hamster toward you will reduce the risk of nibbled fingers.

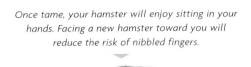

Gaining confidence

Eventually, you will be able to pick up your hamster with one hand, which will make it much easier for you to get him out of his cage. Make sure that your hamster is facing you, with his head toward your wrist (which will also help reduce the risk of nibbled fingers). Then, gently but firmly place your hand around his body, lift him up, and put him on the palm of your other hand. Hamsters have sensitive ears, and your pet will soon become accustomed to the sound of your voice and will soon come to associate you with pleasurable experiences, such as food. You may be able to train your hamster to perform some of his natural actions by rewarding him with treats, but make sure that you don't overfeed him.

Hamsters have a good sense of hearing, and your pet will soon learn to recognize your voice.

HANDLING FOR NERVOUS HAMSTERS OR OWNERS

If you are cautious about handling a new hamster – or need to catch one that is too nervous to be picked up – place an empty jar in front of him. Few hamsters can resist an inviting hideaway, and he will more than likely dive straight in. (If the hamster just pops his head in, you can probably push him the rest of the way.) You can then clap your hand gently over the opening, and your hamster is caught.

If your hamster bites

Most hamsters will only bite when they are frightened, or if they mistake your fingers for food. A few nips in the early days of handling are to be expected: it will take a while for your hamster to recognize your smell. You can minimize the risk of being bitten by washing your hands before touching your pet (to remove any potentially alarming smells) and by keeping his head toward your wrist. Move slowly and learn to recognize when he is frightened.

If your hamster continues to bite, try tapping him very lightly on the nose and saying "no" firmly. Many owners have found that hamsters, as well as dogs, learn to obey such instructions when corrected in this way.

Hamsters love to sit on your arm. Hold your arm against your body and use your other hand to cup the hamster's body. He may be so relaxed he will go to sleep there.

tip

Take off the gloves
Although it is tempting to wear gloves if your hamster has nipped you, doing so will delay the taming process. Your hamster will come to recognize and trust you by the smell of your fingers.

Make sure that you hold your hamster so that he doesn't fall.

Exercise – providing suitable playthings

Hamsters need much more exercise than you might expect. In fact, a hamster can happily run for four or five miles a day if allowed to do so. (It is a good idea to limit his use of an exercise wheel or ball, though, or he may run himself to exhaustion.) Your local pet store will have a selection of

Hamsters enjoy running in an exercise wheel, but ensure that it is used in moderation by removing it from the cage periodically.

different playthings that you can choose for your hamster, but, tempting though it is, don't overcrowd the cage.

Hamster wheels

Some cages come equipped with a treadmill-style wheel, or you can buy one separately. Be aware that a hamster's foot can become trapped in a wheel with bars, so choose a solid wheel.

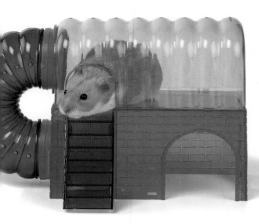

Cage furnishings should provide your hamster with plenty of opportunities to explore, climb, and scramble in and out of inviting holes.

Keep it simple

Don't clutter your hamster's cage with lots of toys. Two or three will be plenty, and you can replace them with others from time to time to keep your pet interested.

Make sure that the wheel is big enough – some sold with a cage are not. If a wheel is too small, the hamster will have to arch his back uncomfortably to run. Also, the hamster's back may rub on the wheel spindle, which can rub the fur away. Male Syrians with long skirts can entangle their coats in the wheel's spindle. Some hamsters can become exercise addicts and can run themselves to exhaustion, so it is best not to keep an exercise wheel in the cage permanently.

offcuts of PVC piping to create hidey-holes for your hamster to explore. They won't last long in the hamster cage, but are easily replaced. Don't forget to provide plenty of wood shavings into which your hamster can burrow, too.

An empty toilet paper roll placed in the cage will provide a cheap, though temporary, tunnel that your hamster will enjoy playing in.

Other toys

All sorts of other playthings are available, including tunnels, see-saws, and miniature houses with doors and windows in and out of which the hamster can climb. Remember that hamsters love climbing and tunneling and look for toys that will provide these opportunities. You can also use toilet paper tubes, empty tissue boxes, and

Playing Outside – safety out of the cage

Your pet will appreciate a change of scenery and the opportunity to explore a greater area, but you will need to take precautions to prevent injury and escapes. It is not a good idea to allow your hamster to play outside of his cage until he has settled into his new home and becomes used to you and to being handled.

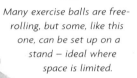

Many exercise balls are free-rolling, but some, like this one, can be set up on a stand – ideal where space is limited.

An exercise ball provides a good way for a hamster to play safely outside his cage, but it should be used only in moderation.

Exercise balls

A ventilated exercise ball will help keep your hamster fit as he rolls around inside it, and it will greatly reduce the risk of injury to your pet when he is out of his cage. However, don't assume that your pet is completely safe just because he is in his ball. Never leave him unattended or near steps, stairs, or an open door. A maximum

Both you and your hamster will enjoy the time he spends out of his cage, but you should never leave him to play unattended.

SIMPLE SAFETY PRECAUTIONS

● Keep doors and windows closed and post a notice on the outside of the door to let other people in the house know that your hamster is loose inside the room.
● Don't let your pet climb too high or run too near the edge of a tabletop – a fall of as little as 3 ft (1 m) can hurt or even kill a hamster.
● Keep electrical cables and house plants (which may be poisonous) out of the reach of your hamster – remember that hamsters are compulsive gnawers.
● Make sure that you keep your hamster well away from steps and stairs, even if he is in his ball.

of 15 minutes is quite enough time for a hamster to play in a ball as he will quickly become tired.

Recapturing escapees

If you can't find or catch a hamster, you can either use a live-trap cage baited with your pet's favorite food, or make your own. Place some bait inside a steep-sided bucket or waste-bin with a ladder or stack of books piled like stairs alongside for access. Once a hamster has scrambled in, he will not be able to scale the steep sides of the bucket to get away again.

Hamsters love to explore, but they are better at climbing up than down, and they have no notion of heights!

tip

Make a play box

Use a large thick cardboard box or plastic storage box to create a safe play area for your pet outside of his cage. You can use clips to hold it in shape so that it can be folded flat and stored when not in use. Include some toys, too, but don't put them too near the sides of the box or your hamster may use them to climb out.

Cage Hygiene – routine maintenance

Hamsters are generally clean animals, and your pet's cage will smell only if you neglect to clean it out. Provided you keep up with daily cleaning tasks (see below), you should only need to clean out the cage once a week. It's a good idea to have a regular routine for this and other maintenance tasks (see page 39).

Your pet is unlikely to appreciate your efforts – hamsters are territorial and use their urine and droppings as markers of their home ownership. Your hamster may try to get in your way or even nip you, but be patient and he will soon grow accustomed to the routine.

Daily housekeeping

When you provide fresh food for your hamster, remove the bowls – one for dry food and one for fresh – from the cage and discard any uneaten food. Wash the bowls in hot soapy water and dry them thoroughly before refilling and replacing them in the cage. Replenish the water bottle, at the same time checking for any leaks or blockages.

Remove any wet bedding and clean out the hamster's "potty" or toilet area, adding fresh wood shavings.

CLEANING THE CAGE

1 Place some wood shavings in a holding cage, and place your hamster inside while you clean his cage. (Alternatively, you could place him in an exercise ball.)

tip

Use safe disinfectants
Household disinfectants are much too strong for hamsters and may burn the skin or cause eye problems. Your pet store will stock suitable pet-safe disinfectant. Read the instructions, and rinse the cage thoroughly after disinfecting.

2 Remove the top of a wire cage and discard the old wood shavings from the base. Use a pet-safe disinfectant to clean the base, making sure that you scrub out corners and rinse and dry it thoroughly. Once the base is completely dry, add plenty of fresh wood shavings.

Save some bedding

tip

If you save a small portion of the soiled bedding and replace it with some fresh bedding, the cage will still smell like home to your hamster and this will reduce the stress associated with cage cleaning.

3 Clean the exercise wheel and any other toys, again using pet-safe disinfectant and rinsing and drying the items thoroughly before replacing them in the cage. Remove and discard your hamster's food hoard, and check his nest box and the bedding inside it, replenishing this with fresh materials as necessary.

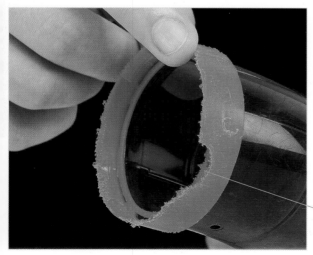

4 This is a good time to check for any damage to the cage and furnishings, thus preventing injury to your pet or his escape. In a wire cage, watch out for rust and sharp edges, and check that the door and catches are secure. In an aquarium-style hamster home, check sealants and inspect the lid for signs of gnawing.

Even fairly robust toys will eventually be destroyed by a hamster. Keep an eye on such items to ensure they are still safe to use.

Grooming and Maintenance

Provided you protect your hamster from injury, feed him properly, and keep his cage clean, he should be quite happy and shouldn't require much maintenance, though long-haired hamsters will require daily brushing. However, it is a good idea to observe your pet's appearance whenever you get him out of his cage. If you know what he looks like normally, you will be better able to spot any problems if and when they arise.

Grooming

Hamsters groom themselves constantly, and short-coated varieties won't need help with this. However, if you have a long-haired hamster, particularly if he's a male, you will need to brush his fur daily to prevent him from becoming matted. Use a suitable brush or comb (your pet store will be able to advise you) and be very gentle. If small tangles do develop, you should be able to gently tease them apart with your fingers. You will need to cut larger mats out with scissors, but be very careful that you don't damage your hamster's delicate skin while doing so.

If you become familiar with the normal appearance of your hamster, you will be better able to spot the symptoms of any health problems.

If your short-haired hamster enjoys being stroked, then you can try introducing gentle brushing sessions, too, using a soft toothbrush. This will do no harm and can help remove bits of residual dust that stick to the fur. It will also help your hamster become accustomed to the process should he need help later in life.

Although short-haired hamsters are quite able to groom themselves, brushing them will do no harm and may encourage tameness. Brush the coat in the direction of growth using a soft toothbrush.

Keep an eye on fur
A sleek coat indicates a healthy hamster; a ruffled, lackluster one is often the first sign of illness.

BATHING HAMSTERS

Bathing a hamster is neither necessary nor advisable unless he gets something sticky in his fur. If you do need to bathe your hamster, fill two bowls with about 2 in (5 cm) of lukewarm water. Wet the hamster in the first bowl, then add a drop or two of baby shampoo to the hamster's fur and rub it in gently, taking care to avoid the eyes. Rinse him in the first bowl, then in the second to make sure all shampoo is removed. Place the hamster in a towel and dry him very carefully. Comb the fur gently to remove any tangles. Make sure that the cage is in a warm room and that the hamster is as dry as possible before you place him back in his cage.

Health Care – symptoms and cures

However carefully you look after your hamster, he may succumb to illness or be injured. Check your hamster regularly for any signs of ill health – ideally, whenever you get him out of his cage. Inspect his eyes, nose, bottom, and general appearance at least once a week and his teeth, and nails at least once a month. The diagnostic chart on the following pages will provide advice on what you can do and when you need to enlist the help of your veterinarian. Remember that your local pet store may also be able to give you advice on simple treatments.

WHAT TO LOOK FOR

Fur – Some loss is usual in old age, but in young hamsters it could indicate a problem. The coat should be sleek.

Body – Check for unusual lumps and bumps. Notice any weight loss.

Eyes – Check for foreign bodies or weeping.

Nose – A wet or runny nose could indicate a cold or allergy.

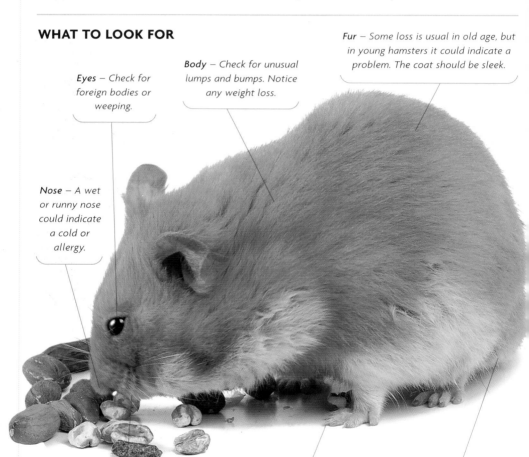

Teeth – Make sure they are wearing down correctly. If they overgrow, they will need to be trimmed by a vet.

Nails – On some species, they grow very fast and will need regular trimming.

Bottom – It should be dry. Never ignore any indication of diarrhea or wet tail.

When you get your hamster out of his cage, examine his body to check that no lumps or bumps have appeared.

Most injuries are the result of falls, and your hamster is likely to suffer from shock. Place the cage in a warm, dark place and check on him every few hours. If you suspect he has broken a limb, you will need to take your pet to see a veterinarian. Wash small cuts and bites with a weak antiseptic solution.

Colds and heat stroke

In cold weather, hamsters are susceptible to catching colds from humans. Keep your hamster warm and, if symptoms persist, treat with antibiotics, which you can obtain from your veterinarian. (Follow the instructions carefully.)

In hot weather, you will need to make sure that your hamster's cage has sufficient ventilation and shade. If your hamster collapses, twitching and trembling, he may be suffering from heat stroke. You will need to act swiftly to move his cage to a cooler place, but he

Check under the tail for soiling, and never ignore any indication of diarrhea or wet tail.

should then recover quite quickly. Both problems can be prevented to some extent by making sure that you have located the cage away from windows, doors, and radiators or other heat sources (see page 26).

DIAGNOSING AND TREATING HEALTH PROBLEMS

Symptoms	Likely causes	Treatment
Wet or runny nose	Cold or flu (hamsters susceptible to catching colds from humans).	Keep hamster warm. If symptoms worsen, antibiotics may be needed.
	An allergy (some hamsters can be irritated by dusty wood shavings or strong smelling dyes in bedding).	Use dust-extracted shavings and bedding and foods that contain no colored dyes.
Watery eyes	Foreign body in the eye caused by burrowing in bedding.	Wipe the eye with a cotton ball and clean water. If the eye has been damaged, seek veterinary advice.
	If eye is also swollen and there is no evidence of a foreign body, cause could be glaucoma.	No cure for glaucoma. Some veterinarians suggest removal of affected eye.
Bluish circle in center of eye	Sign of cataracts in an older hamster.	No cure. The hamster will lose his sight, but can still lead a happy life.
Diarrhea	Stress (particularly in new and/or very young hamsters). Too much green food.	Avoid feeding all green foods until diarrhea stops, then reintroduce them again slowly.
	A bacterial infection called wet tail (another symptom is an unpleasant smelling discharge).	Seek veterinary advice. Antibiotics will be needed.
Discharge from the vulva	A womb or ovary problem – common in older females.	Seek veterinary advice. Antibiotics and/or hysterectomy will be needed.
Fur loss and/or red or raw skin	Could be symptomatic of mites, allergies, or kidney disease. (Some fur loss is usual in older hamsters).	Seek veterinary advice.
	Cushing's disease can cause fur loss and sore, thickened skin.	No cure, but seek veterinary advice.

Lumps or bumps on the body	Irregular hard lumps can indicate a tumor.	Many lumps are noncancerous and can be removed by a veterinarian under anesthesia.
	A fluid-feeling lump may be a cyst.	Needs draining by a veterinarian.
	A soft lump that may look creamy pale may be an abscess. Abscesses can develop as a result of a wound or bite.	Needs draining by a veterinarian.
Skin wounds or bites	Caused by fighting between hamsters living together.	Separate hamsters if squabbling is serious. Seek veterinary advice for serious wounds. Tea tree cream can be used on minor ones.
Excessive urination	Bladder infection	Antibiotics can be administered by your veterinarian.
	Diabetes (Russian Dwarf Campbell hamsters are particularly prone to this).	No cure; however, you can keep your hamster comfortable by keeping him cool and never letting him run out of water.
Difficulty urinating	Bladder stones or blockages	Seek veterinary advice.

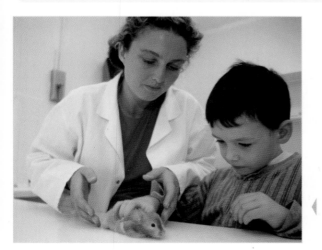

tip

Don't let your pet suffer

The average life span of a hamster is only about two years, and very old hamsters may quite suddenly become feeble and gaunt. If your pet appears to be suffering, it is kinder to take him to the vet, who will be able to grant him a quick, humane death.

Although many common health problems can be treated with antibiotics available from your pet store, it's always a good idea to consult a vet before administering treatment.

Developing Your Hobby

Learning more, hamster shows, and breeding advice

*Once you have kept your hamster for a while, you may decide
that you would like to expand your interest in the hobby and take
on some new challenges. You may want to think about keeping one
or more of the other species of hamster – one of the dwarf species
that may be more difficult to maintain than a Syrian hamster. Or
you may decide to visit a hamster show and perhaps enter your pet.
You may even want to think about breeding hamsters, though make
sure you have found good homes for the babies first.*

Making contact with others

While you can gain more information about your new hobby from reading other books, magazines, and websites, it helps to know other hobbyists who may have more experience in keeping hamsters. The best way to do this is to join a hamster club. If you don't know of one in your area, contact your national hamster association, which will be able to advise you.

Most hamster clubs have their own websites, which will provide you with access to the latest information on hamster shows and new varieties. They will also be able to give advice on hamster care and breeding, as well as put you in touch with other hobbyists.

Hamster shows

Most hamster shows have a special section for pet hamsters as well as ones for Syrian and Dwarf (Other Species) hamsters. In the pet section, hamsters are judged on tameness and condition, which is not necessarily the same as appearance: the judges will be looking primarily to see that the hamster is in good health and has been well looked after.

You don't need to be a member of a club to exhibit your hamster in the pet class, nor do you need to enter your pet in advance. Most clubs will be happy for you to just visit a show and to ask questions without entering your hamster.

The Syrian and Dwarf (or Other Species) sections will usually be divided into three main categories: straight class, duplicate class, and nonstandard class. In the first of these, similar hamsters are measured against each other; the duplicate class

allows different hamster varieties to be judged against each other. Most duplicate classes have sections for novices, juniors, and breeders. Hamsters that don't conform to a standard color will be entered in the appropriate nonstandard class.

A dwarf hamster in his show pen. The red spot on top of the hamster's pen indicates that he is the winner in his class.

MARKING CRITERIA

Shows in most countries will follow the same marking systems, but allocation of marks may vary slightly. Categories may be as follows:

- Color and markings
- Type
- Fur
- Size
- Condition
- Ears and eyes

Breeding Hamsters

The decision to breed hamsters is not one you should make without good reason and without some experience in keeping hamsters. If you do decide to breed, make sure that you use only healthy animals and that you know what you are going to do with the litter – there are already more hamsters being bred than there are good homes for them.

These four-day-old baby hamsters are blind and bare, but they already have tiny teeth and whiskers

Introducing male and female

Hamsters breed more readily in the summer months, and females come into season about every four days. Use a separate "honeymoon" cage to introduce the pair to each other, allowing each to spend time in the cage alone first so that they are accustomed to each other's scent. Put the male in the honeymoon cage, then introduce the female in the evening. Be ready to separate them – wearing gloves – if fighting occurs. If the female is ready to mate, she will stand still, lower her back, and put her tail in the air. This freezing position will indicate she is ready to be mated. The pair will usually mate several times in quick succession, after which you should remove the female.

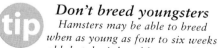 

At 16 days old, these baby hamsters are covered with hair and their eyes have opened.

Don't breed youngsters
Hamsters may be able to breed when as young as four to six weeks old, but don't breed hamsters less than six months old, as early pregnancy will stunt a female's growth.

Rearing baby hamsters

A Syrian female will carry her young for 16 days; the gestation period for Campbell, Winter White, and Chinese hamsters is 18 days and for Roborovski hamsters about 21 days. While she is pregnant, you will need to supply your hamster with extra food, and increased rations should continue until she has weaned her litter. The average litter size is about four to six for dwarf species and eight to twelve for a Syrian, but there may be only one or as many as twenty babies. They will be born blind, naked, and helpless. Don't disturb the nest at this stage or the mother may kill and eat her babies. It won't be long

before the babies surface, though it will be a couple of weeks before they can open their eyes. At this stage, you can begin handling them to encourage them to become hand-tamed.

Baby hamsters grow very quickly and will need plenty of food. By the time they are about three weeks old, they will be fully weaned, and you will need to remove the mother and separate the babies into single-sex groups. They will be ready to move to their new homes at six weeks old.

At six weeks old, young hamsters are ready to be moved to their new homes.

Young hamsters need to have food available to them all the time to support their fast growth.

CAUTION: WHITE-BELLIED GENE

Some hamsters with white fur on their bellies – and all those with a roan coat – are carriers of the anophthalmic gene. Mating two such carriers together can produce offspring with no eyes. So unless you are sure that your hamsters are not carriers, do not breed them.

PROJECT TEAM

Editor: Mary Grangeia
Design: Patti Escabi

T.F.H. PUBLICATIONS

President/CEO: Glen S. Axelrod
Executive Vice President: Mark E. Johnson
Publisher: Christopher T. Reggio
Production Manager: Kathy Bontz

T.F.H. PUBLICATIONS, INC.

One TFH Plaza
Third and Union Avenues
Neptune City, NJ 0773

CLUBS

American Hamster Association
P.O. Box 203, Chapin, SC 29036, US

British Hamster Association
P.O. Box 825, Sheffield, S17 3RU, England

PICTURE CREDITS

The majority of the pictures in this book were taken by Neil Sutherland and are the copyright of Interpet Publishing. Other pictures are also the copyright of Interpet Publishing, with the exception of the following: pages 30(L), 34 and 46: William Watling/www.illuminessence.co.uk); pages 44 and 59: RSPCA photo library (Angela Hampton).

The publisher would like to thank Newman and Bloodworths Pet Shop, Cheltenham for supplying the cage and hamster shown on page 34.